Z is for Zombie

Myths and legends from around the world

Written and illustrated by
Lorri Lambert

Balboa Press books may be ordered through booksellers or by contacting:

Balboa Press
A Division of Hay House
1663 Liberty Drive
Bloomington, IN 47403
www.balboapress.com.au
AU TFN: 1 800 844 925 (Toll Free inside Australia)
AU Local: 0283 107 086 (+61 2 8310 7086 from outside Australia)

ISBN: 978-1-5043-2304-8 (sc)
ISBN: 978-1-5043-2303-1 (e)

Print information available on the last page.

Balboa Press rev. date: 10/26/2020

BALBOA.PRESS
A DIVISION OF HAY HOUSE

About the book

Storytelling is an important part of all cultures, and stories are an important part of cultural identity. This book recognises and celebrates living in a global community and all the richness this has brought to our lives but in a whimsical and fun way.

A wide range of mythological creatures and objects have been selected, including a few well known favourites. The book can be read on two levels. Firstly, as a simple ABC of characters for those who want to introduce children to mythology and fantasy or secondly as a bit more complex book by including a short description of each creature.

About the author

Lorri Lambert lives on a couple of hectares in rural Australia with her extended family and a few chooks. She has been fascinated by stories, myths, and legends since first reading Aesop's Fables as a child. Lorri is an avid reader of fantasy stories, and an artist who often paints fantasy creatures, especially dragons.

This book was inspired by her children who also share her love of the fantastic and who have kept her lifelong passion of storytelling alive by reading to their children every night.

Dedication:

For my beautiful grandchildren who love coming on adventures with me.

Disclaimer:

A a   Antmen (Greece)

As big as a person and knows how to fight

Similar to army ants, they were human size. They could carry and use four weapons at a time and use their large eyes to see In all directions at once.

B b Bunyip (Australia)

Hides in the billabong and comes out at night

It is said that bunyips lurk in swamps, billabongs, and rivers. The origin of the word bunyip has been traced to the Wemba–Wemba or Wergaia language of the Aboriginal people of Victoria, in South Eastern Australia

C c Castle (Many cultures)

Strong and sturdy, a place to hold feasts

There are many different types of castles, palaces and strongholds. They are big strong structures built for lords, ladies, kings, and queens to protect their lands with their armies.

D d   Dragon (Many cultures)

Friend or foe they are mighty beasts

Most cultures have their own tales and stories about these spectacular creatures. Dragons usually look a bit like snakes or lizards but are more beautiful and magical.

E e Ettin (England)

A big brutish beast with one head or two

A giant or ogre so huge it can pull trees from the ground and use them as weapons. In some legends they may even have three heads.

F f Far Darrig (Ireland)

A man dressed in red who plays tricks on you

His name means "The red man", as he always dresses in red. They are known to be dreadful tricksters with pointy ears and wild hair.

G g   Gryphon (Greece and Italy)

Part lion, part eagle it flies through the skies

This creature has the body, tail and legs of a lion, the head and wings of an eagle. Gryphons were known for guarding treasures and priceless possessions

H h Hydra (Greece)

It has lots of heads and too many eyes

The Hydra is a snake like creature with many heads and in some stories every time a head is chopped off, two new heads would grow.

I i Ikaroa (New Zealand)

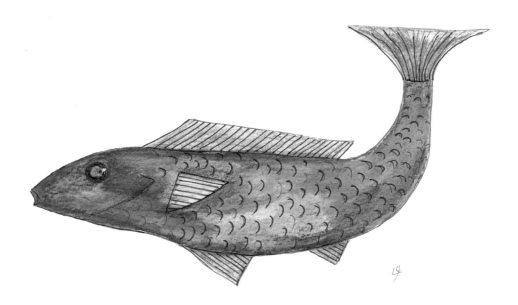

This fish made the stars in our own milky way

In Maori stories Ikaroa is the long fish that gave birth to all the stars in the Milky Way. The stars are believed to be ornaments of the Sky God.

J j Jinn (Arabia)

He lives in a lamp and then comes out to play

Featured in the *One Thousand and One Nights*, a collection of Middle Eastern folk tales. The Jinn, also known as a Genie, can be summoned and bound to grant wishes. But care must be taken as they can be treacherous.

K k Kelpie (Scotland)

It lives in the water and plays without cares

A kelpie is a Shape changing water spirit. Kelpies are said to live in rivers and streams and usually look like a horse. Beware though as they might try to take you away into the watery depths.

Guarding the forest, the wolves, and the bears

A spirit who rules over the forest and hunters. They can appear as an element of the forest and can change into an animal, a tree, or a mushroom, as well as be a mix of a human and animal or plant.

M m Mothman (North America)

This weird flying beast has wings that go swish

A new myth based on sightings of this creature near Point Pleasant, West Virginnia, USA in 1960's. He is a winged, humanoid creature with bright red eyes and wings like a moth.

N n Ningyo (Japan)

A strange little mermaid with teeth like a fish

Described as having a monkey's mouth with small teeth like a fish, shining golden scales, and a quiet, musical voice. Catching a ningyo was believed to bring storms and misfortune. A ningyo washed onto the beach was an omen of war or calamity.

O o Ogopogo (Canada)

The lake is its home and it has many humps

Ogopogo is often described as dark and Multi humped, with green, black, brown, or gray skin. Its head can look like a snake, sheep, horse, seal or even an alligator.

P p Pixiu (China)

A guardian lion, to attention it jumps

This strong, winged creature has the head of a dragon and body of a lion. Pixiu is a guardian and powerful protector and is believed to bring wealth and good fortune.

This colourful serpent has feathers and wings

Quetzalcoatl was related to gods of the Wind and the dawn. He was also the patron god of the Aztec priesthood, of learning, merchants and of arts, crafts, and knowledge.

R r Roc (many cultures)

A gigantic bird, feared by sailors and kings

It was said that this gigantic bird could carry off elephants and other large beasts for food and is featured in Arabic folklore. The Venetian traveler Marco Polo believes he saw one when exploring near Madagascar, an island off the coast of Eastern Africa.

S s   Skeleton (many cultures)

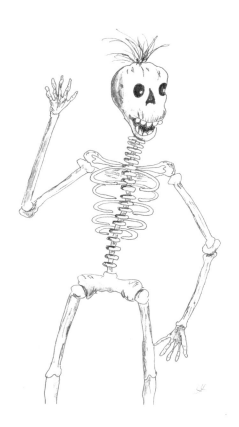

A thing made of bones it rattles about

A skeleton is a type of undead creature often found in fantasy and horror fiction. Most are human skeletons, but they can also be skeletal creatures.

Tt Tokoloshe (South Africa)

This small cheeky sprite is really a lout

A small, hairy creature, this mischievous sprite can become invisible by drinking water or swallowing a stone. Tokoloshe are often called upon to cause trouble for others. They also love to drink milk.

A beautiful beast that grants wishes, its true

Unicorns are usually depicted as white, Horse like creatures with a single horn growing from its forehead that is long and straight, marked with spirals. Unicorns are said to have magical powers and can grant wishes.

V v Vardøger (Norway)

A ghostly person who looks just like you

The ghostly double mimics the voice, scent, or appearance of a real person. Sometimes called a doppelganger, the ghostly double is usually seen or heard just before the person arrives.

Part person, part beast with sharp teeth and claws

In Somalia, there is a tale of a man who could transform himself into a "hyena–man" by rubbing himself with a magic stick at nightfall and he could return to his human state before dawn.

X x   Xana (Spain)

A beautiful maiden that lives by the shores

A creature of extraordinary beauty believed to live in fountains, rivers, waterfalls or forested regions with pure water. She has long blonde hair, which she tends to with gold or silver combs woven from sun or moonbeams.

Y y Yggdrasil (Norse)

A mighty tree, standing strong and proud

In old Norse mythology there are nine worlds. All are connected via the roots and branches of this huge tree. It is sometimes called the tree of life and while it remains healthy all the worlds will thrive.

Z z   Zombie (Haiti)

He wants to eat brains, but he's just not allowed

Zombies first appeared in Haiti in the 17th and 18th centuries, when the country was ruled by France, and had African slaves brought in to work on sugar plantations. Zombies are undead, mindless slaves that crave flesh and brains of the living.

Resources:

https://latgale.academy/mythological-creatures/
http://bestiary.ca/index.html
https://norse-mythology.org/
https://www.supersummary.com/folklore-mythology-guide/
https://mythology.wikia.org/

Printed in the United States
By Bookmasters